It's Another Ace Book from CGP

It's chock-full of questions that are carefully designed to make sure you know all the really important stuff about 'Micro-organisms & Reversible Changes' in Year Six Science.

And we've had a really good stab at making it funny — so you'll actually want to use it.

Simple as that.

CGP are just the best

The central aim of Coordination Group Publications is to produce top quality books that are carefully written, beautifully presented and marvellously funny — whilst always making sure they exactly cover the National Curriculum for each subject.

And then we supply them to as many people as we possibly can, as cheaply as we possibly can.

Buy our books — they're ace

Contents

Micro-organisms

Germs and Diseases 1
Micro-Organisms in Your Mouth 3
Food Decay 4
Food Hygiene 5
Decay Can Be Helpful 6
Micro-organisms Cause Decay 7
Yeast Feeds and Grows 8
Useful Micro-organisms 10
Revision — Micro-organisms 12

Reversible Changes

Adding Solids to Water 13
Adding Solids to Other Liquids 15
Separating Mixtures 16
Mixes Involving Irreversible Reactions 18
Changes due to Heating 20
Changes due to Cooling 21
Burning Makes New Materials 22
Burning is Dangerous 24
Revision — Reversible Changes 25
Index 26

Answers to the questions are on the back of the Pull-out Poster in the centre of the book.

Published by Coordination Group Publications Ltd.

Contributors:
Angela Billington BA (Hons), MPhil
Chris Dennett   BSc (Hons)
Lindsay Jordan BSc (Hons)
Tim Major
Katherine Stewart BA (Hons)
Claire Thompson BSc
Tim Wakeling   BA (Hons), GIMA
James Paul Wallis   BEng (Hons)
Suzanne Worthington BSc (Hons)

ISBN 1-84146-276-4
Groovy website: www.cgpbooks.co.uk
Jolly bits of clipart from CorelDRAW
Printed by Elanders Hindson, Newcastle upon Tyne.

Text, design, layout and original illustrations © Coordination Group Publications Ltd. 2000
All rights reserved.

Germs and Diseases

Diseases are horrible things and they're caused by tiny things called <u>germs</u>. You can't <u>see</u> germs — so it's difficult to avoid them. This page is about how people found out that germs cause disease. Have a read of this article and answer the questions.

> Edward Jenner was a British doctor born in 1749. When he was alive, the disease smallpox was a big problem, killing lots of people. Cowpox was a similar but less serious disease that was spread by cows. Jenner noticed that people who had suffered from cowpox seemed to be immune to smallpox. To test this idea, he injected people with cowpox and, sure enough, it protected them against smallpox.
>
> Jenner believed that smallpox was spread by a tiny micro-organism he called a virus. Lots of scientists at that time knew that germs existed, but they hadn't realised that they caused disease — in fact, some even thought that diseases *produced* germs.
>
> Louis Pasteur, a French chemist born in 1822, was the one who finally figured out the real connection between germs and disease. Pasteur began by investigating the problem of sour wine. He discovered that germs from the air had got into the liquid and contaminated it, making it spoil and go sour. Pasteur realised that if germs from the air could do this to wine, they could also infect people and animals, causing disease.
>
> Pasteur spent years testing this theory and disproving the belief that most scientists held — that the outbreak of disease happened spontaneously with no cause at all. The experiments he carried out proved that germs are tiny micro-organisms that cause decay and disease. This research led to the discovery of <u>vaccines</u> for many fatal diseases — they work in the same way that Jenner's cowpox injections protected people against smallpox.

What some words in this article mean:
immune — you can't catch a certain disease
micro-organism — very small organisms which can be harmful
contaminate — when one substance gets something else in it that changes it and shouldn't be there
spontaneous — happening without warning

Q1 Why did Jenner think that infecting people with cowpox would stop them getting smallpox?

....

Q2 What did Jenner think caused smallpox? ....

Q3 What did many scientists in Louis Pasteur's time think caused disease?

....

Q4 What did Pasteur think caused disease? ....

Q5 What did Pasteur's experiments prove that germs are?

....

<u>If smallpox was bad — what would bigpox be like?</u>

<u>Scientific evidence</u> proved that diseases don't just happen all on their own — they are caused by <u>germs</u>. Germs are very small <u>organisms</u> which carry disease from one thing to the next — gross.

Germs and Diseases

Germs are carried in the air and on things you touch. They can be passed on by animals and by other people. If germs get into your lungs or stomach, they can make you ill, but there are loads of things you can do to stop them.

Q1 Here are a few ways diseases can be spread. For each picture, choose the best way of preventing the germs from spreading and write it out on the dotted lines.

a) Sneezing or coughing on people can spread disease. This can be prevented by ....

Taking vitamin pills
Using a hankie

b) Eating food with dirty hands can make you ill. This can be prevented by ....

Washing your hands before you eat
Becoming a vegetarian

c) Sometimes food contains bacteria which can make you ill. This can be prevented by ....
....

Only eating green vegetables
Washing everything before you eat it
Making sure things are cooked properly

d) Some insects carry germs in their blood which can infect you if you are bitten. This can be prevented by .... and ....

Using insect repellent
Wearing long clothing
Biting the insect back

Q2 Use the words from the green boxes to fill in the blanks in this paragraph about chickenpox.

If you catch chickenpox, you get covered in itchy

.... Chickenpox is a disease caused by a

micro-organism that can .... get from person

to person. .... and ....

are other highly infectious ....

Yet again Arthur woke up covered in spots.

spots | easily | diseases | mumps | measles

Chickenpox isn't hard to spot...

There are lots of ways that germs get about — from coughs or sneezes, from uncooked meat or food that's been kept too long... When you think about it, it's amazing you can avoid 'em at all.

Micro-Organisms in Your Mouth

Your mouth is wet and warm and sometimes has tiny bits of food hidden in the corners — bacteria <u>love</u> it. Micro-organisms cause <u>tooth decay</u> and <u>gum disease</u> — that's why you have to get rid of the little blighters.

Q1 Fill in the gaps to finish off this paragraph about tooth decay.

After a meal or snack, sugar is left in your mouth. The sugar is eaten by .... The bacteria form a sticky slime covering your teeth called .... This contains .... , which rots away your tooth enamel and weakens your teeth.

(ACID)   (PLAQUE)   (BACTERIA)

Using dental floss is a good way to keep teeth healthy.

Q2 Each of these pictures shows something you can do to keep your teeth healthy. Match them up to the descriptions below by putting the right letter in each box.

B Using this twice a day, with toothpaste, helps to remove plaque and bits of food which bacteria feed on.

D These make your teeth grow long and pointy so you can scare your friends.

F Doing this regularly will make sure that any decay is treated quickly and your teeth will get a proper clean if they need it.

H You can swill this around your mouth. It kills bacteria and contains fluoride, which helps to keep teeth strong.

A Using this will make all your teeth nice and straight.

C Using this helps to remove plaque and bits of food from <u>between</u> your teeth.

E You put this on your toothbrush. It contains fluoride to help keep your teeth strong.

G Doing this will make sure all your teeth fall out while you're asleep.

I Avoiding these will decrease the amount of sugar left in your mouth.

Now, here's a page to get your teeth into...

Looking after your teeth is pretty easy — spend a couple of minutes to <u>brush</u> them in the morning and in the evening, and go to the <u>dentist</u> regularly for a <u>check-up</u>. No big deal.

Food Decay

You'll love this page — it's all about <u>mould</u>. Mouldy food is smelly and horrible, which is a good way of telling it's <u>not</u> OK to eat — if you ate it, you might get <u>ill</u>.

Q1 What has made these foods go mouldy? (Circle) the right answer.

The foods have been washed recently.

Micro-organisms are feeding on them.

The foods have been put in the freezer.

A magic spell has been put on the foods.

Q2 Sanjeev left these four slices of bread in different places, with labels on them. After ten days, they looked like this.

a) Where was the best place to keep bread for a long time?

....

b) Why do you think this place stops mould growing?

....

Fridge 3°C Breadbin 12°C
Freezer -4°C Table 18°C

Q3 a) These four pictures show the same loaf of bread on different days. Write 'fresh', 'two days', 'four days' or 'eight days' next to each loaf, to show how old it is.

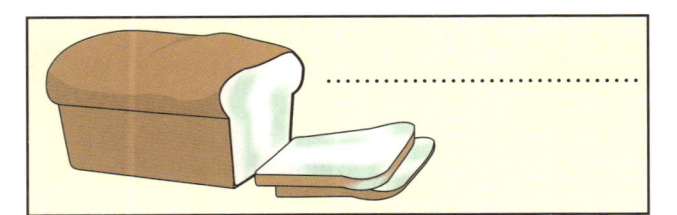

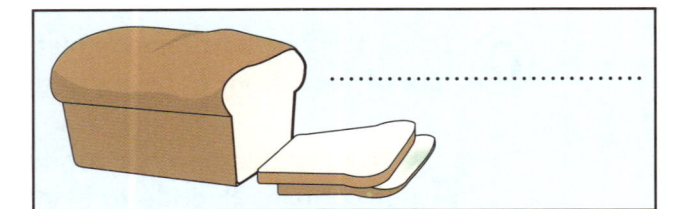

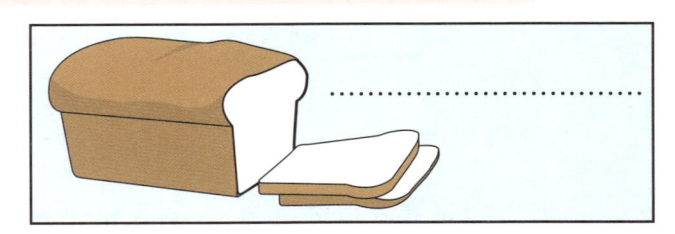

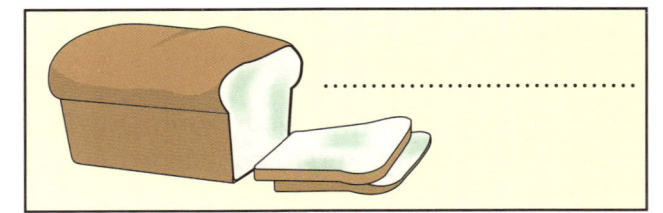

b) In this box, draw the bread as it would look after six days. Try to use the same colours as the pictures above.

The bread's off — it's had the red card...

The green or blue mouldy bits on food are where micro-organisms are <u>growing</u> and <u>reproducing</u> — and eating the food to help them do this. It'd be a <u>seriously</u> bad idea for you to eat mouldy food.

Food Hygiene

Food hygiene is all about doing sensible things to keep those evil micro-organisms away.

Q1 Here are some ways to <u>stop</u> or <u>slow down</u> food decay, and the <u>reasons</u> why they work. In each box, write A, B, C or D to show why the method works. (Use some letters twice.)

- Put the food in the freezer ☐
- Put the food in a tin ☐
- Put the food in the fridge ☐
- Put the food in airtight packaging ☐
- Pickle the food ☐
- Dry the food ☐

A Micro-organisms can't grow or reproduce because air can't get in.

B Micro-organisms can't grow or reproduce well in the vinegar, because it's too acidic.

C Micro-organisms can only grow and reproduce slowly because it's cold.

D Micro-organisms can't grow or reproduce because there's no water.

Q2 Complete these sentences about how to handle food using words from the green mould.

Use .... knives for cooked and raw meat, and keep cooked and .... meat apart in the fridge. This stops .... from spreading to the cooked meat. Cook food thoroughly to kill any micro-organisms. .... your hands before you handle food, so micro-organisms don't get from your hands to the food.

Don't eat .... food — it can give you food poisoning.

words: wash, micro-organisms, different, mouldy, raw

Q3 Alice put some sandwiches in her locker and forgot about them over the holidays. When term started again, the sandwiches were green and fluffy.

a) What should Alice do with the sandwiches?

....

b) What could she do to the locker to stop micro-organisms spreading to her new sandwiches? Tick the right answer.

- Eat the sandwiches. ☐
- Take away the old sandwiches and clean the locker. ☐
- Run away. ☐

Alice's sandwiches had changed a bit since she last looked.

"Oh crumbs..."

Hygiene — what Jean's mates always say...

Watch out for the 'Use by' date on food. <u>Don't</u> eat the food after that date, because it could be off. Sometimes you get a 'Sell by' date instead — shops aren't allowed to sell food after this date.

Decay Can Be Helpful

Decay isn't just about bad things like tooth decay and rotting fruit. It's really <u>useful</u> for some things.

Q1 This seagull is looking at what decays in this rubbish tip. He's recording his results in these blue boxes. Draw in the pictures where he's missed them, and write in whether the thing decays or not where he's missed that.

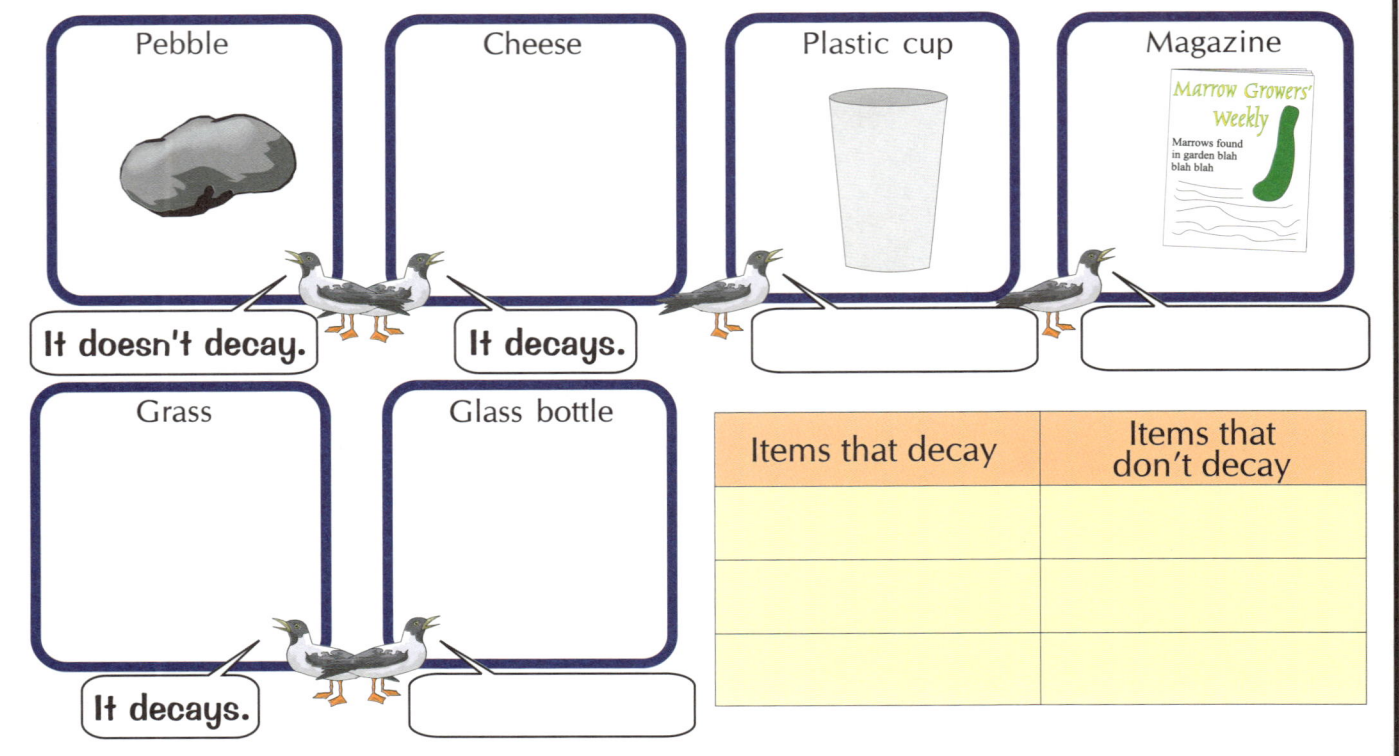

Pebble	Cheese	Plastic cup	Magazine
It doesn't decay.	It decays.		

Grass	Glass bottle
It decays.	

Items that decay	Items that don't decay

Q2 What will happen to the objects below if they are left in the rubbish tip? Put a tick in the box if it DECAYS or a cross if it DOESN'T DECAY.

Use the table above for help.

- Broken glass bottle ☐
- Roses ☐
- Banana ☐
- Plastic toy helicopter ☐
- Huge gold bar ☐
- Newspaper ☐

What do you think of this stuff so far?

This page isn't great — it's rotten...

Not all rubbish is chucked into a tip — glass, paper, metals and plastic can be <u>collected</u> and turned into new things. Leftover bits of some types of food can be made into <u>compost</u> to feed plants.

Micro-organisms Cause Decay

So, guess why I'm going on about <u>decay</u> when this is a book about <u>micro-organisms</u>.
Yep — it's because decay is <u>caused</u> by micro-organisms.

Q1 Fill in the gaps in this paragraph about micro-organisms using some of the words from the bin.

Bin words: disappear, feed, nutrients, beasts, microbes, enlarge, run out, oxygen, decay

Micro-organisms or .... cause .... The micro-organisms that cause it .... on materials that are decaying. Just like when you eat a meal, any lump of decaying material will eventually .... That's what happens when the decaying material is completely decomposed, and there's nothing left.

> Most plastics don't decay, but there are special <u>biodegradable plastics</u> which do. Lots of companies now make their packaging from biodegradable plastic so that it will eventually disappear.

Q2 Imagine what life would be like if nothing decayed.
Give one reason why it's a good thing that stuff decays.

....
....
....

List:
Jumbo clothes peg
Cap
T-Shirt

The rubbish tip workers had a surprising item.

Landfills
Rubbish from your home is taken to a landfill site. Landfill rubbish tips produce methane gas. When some landfills are full, they are covered with grass and the gas is trapped. Then it's piped away to be released into the air — or it can be burnt for heating.

Q3 Read the information above about landfill rubbish tips, and then put a big ⓡing around the sentence below that explains where the methane comes from.

| Water dissolves plastics in the tip. The plastic mixes with water to make methane gas. | Micro-organisms feed on the rubbish, making it decay. One of the waste products is methane. | Vegetables contain methane. When they are broken up in the tip, it is released. |

I got a grade D in music — I'm a D composer...

There you go, then — decay happens when things are <u>eaten</u> by <u>micro-organisms</u>. That's what happens to things like bits of old pizza when you throw them away and they get taken to a dump.

Yeast Feeds and Grows

Usually, you don't want micro-organisms to grow — but yeast is a micro-organism that you do want to grow, because you use it to make lovely tasty bread. Or even grotty, horrible bread.

Q1 Steven has been making bread dough from flour, sugar and water. The first batch was made with yeast, and the second batch was made without yeast. The first batch rose.

a) What was in the first batch of bread that made it rise? ....

b) The bread that rose had lots of tiny bubbles of gas in it. Circle the sentence that explains where the gas bubbles came from.

| The gas bubbles appear from nowhere. | The yeast produces gas bubbles as it grows. | The flour produces the gas bubbles by breathing. |

Q2 I'm doing an investigation to see what yeast needs in order to grow. I want to know if it needs heat and if it needs sugar. Tick one box from each pair, so that the experiment will work.

a) I should use only one bowl of dough. ☐ OR I should use four bowls of dough for comparison. ☐

b) Two bowls should be left in a warm place (like an airing cupboard), and two in a cold place (like a fridge). ☐ OR All the bowls should be left in a warm place. ☐

c) I shouldn't add sugar to any of the bowls. ☐ OR One of each pair of bowls should have sugar added, and one shouldn't have any sugar added. ☐

d) I should check the bowls after a day to see if the dough has risen. ☐ OR I should leave the bowls alone and not bother checking on them. ☐

Steven wondered if he'd put a little bit too much yeast into his dough.

My dough's been promoted — it'll get a rise...

Bread rises because yeast is growing. When yeast grows it produces bubbles of gas — but it won't do it just anywhere. It only grows under certain conditions — head onto the next page.

Yeast Feeds and Grows

Just like any other <u>living</u> thing, yeast needs a few things in order to <u>grow</u>. It'll need some kind of <u>food</u> for a start.

Q1 These pictures show what happened in my experiment from page 8. Put a tick under each picture if the dough has risen — and then write HAS RISEN or HASN'T RISEN in the right places in the table.

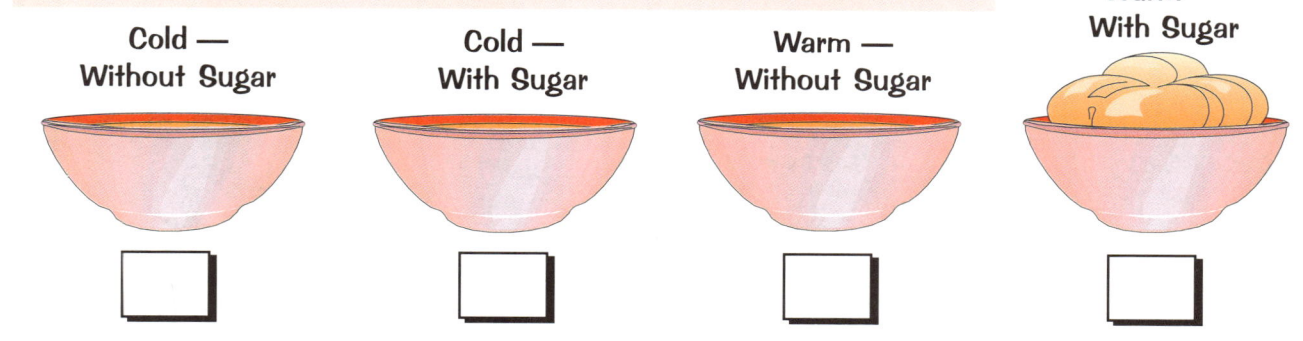

Cold — Without Sugar   Cold — With Sugar   Warm — Without Sugar   Warm — With Sugar

☐   ☐   ☐   ☐

	Warm	Cold
Sugar	....	....
No Sugar	....	....

Lucy wondered if eating yeast would make her grow a bit faster.

Q2 Using the table, write down the two things yeast needs in order to grow. ....

Q3 Fill in the gaps in these sentences using some of the words from the loaf of bread.

Yeast needs .... in order to grow, and it also needs to be in a .... place. Yeast can use sugar as its food. Because yeast grows, we know that it is .... Most living things need food and warmth in order to live and ....

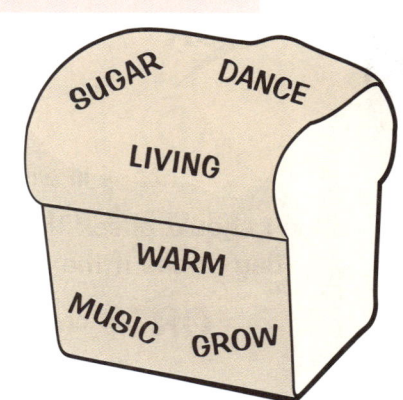

Loaf of bread words: SUGAR, DANCE, LIVING, WARM, MUSIC, GROW

Dough's favourite programme — Yeastenders...

Yeast isn't so very different from <u>you</u>. OK, I admit it <u>looks</u> a bit different from you, and hopefully you don't <u>smell</u> quite like it. But like you it needs warmth and food or it won't do anything useful.

Useful Micro-Organisms

Micro-organisms can be dangerous and harmful when they cause <u>disease</u>, but they can also be really <u>useful</u>. We use them for loads of things, like making some kinds of <u>food</u>.

Q1 Fill in the gaps in this paragraph using some of the words from the cloud underneath.

Micro-organisms can be really useful in different ways. People can use them to .... food. Others, called ...., help dead plants and animals to decay (.....................). Special .... are okay to eat, and are used to make yoghurt and .... Bread dough only rises if you use ....

Bertie loved working at the factory with the other bacteria.

Word cloud: CHEESE, DECOMPOSERS, PHONES, BACTERIA, ROT, MAKE, SALT, YEAST, COFFEE

Q2 Here are some pictures of some micro-organisms at work. Think about whether they are helpful or not, and then write HELPFUL or UNHELPFUL next to each one.

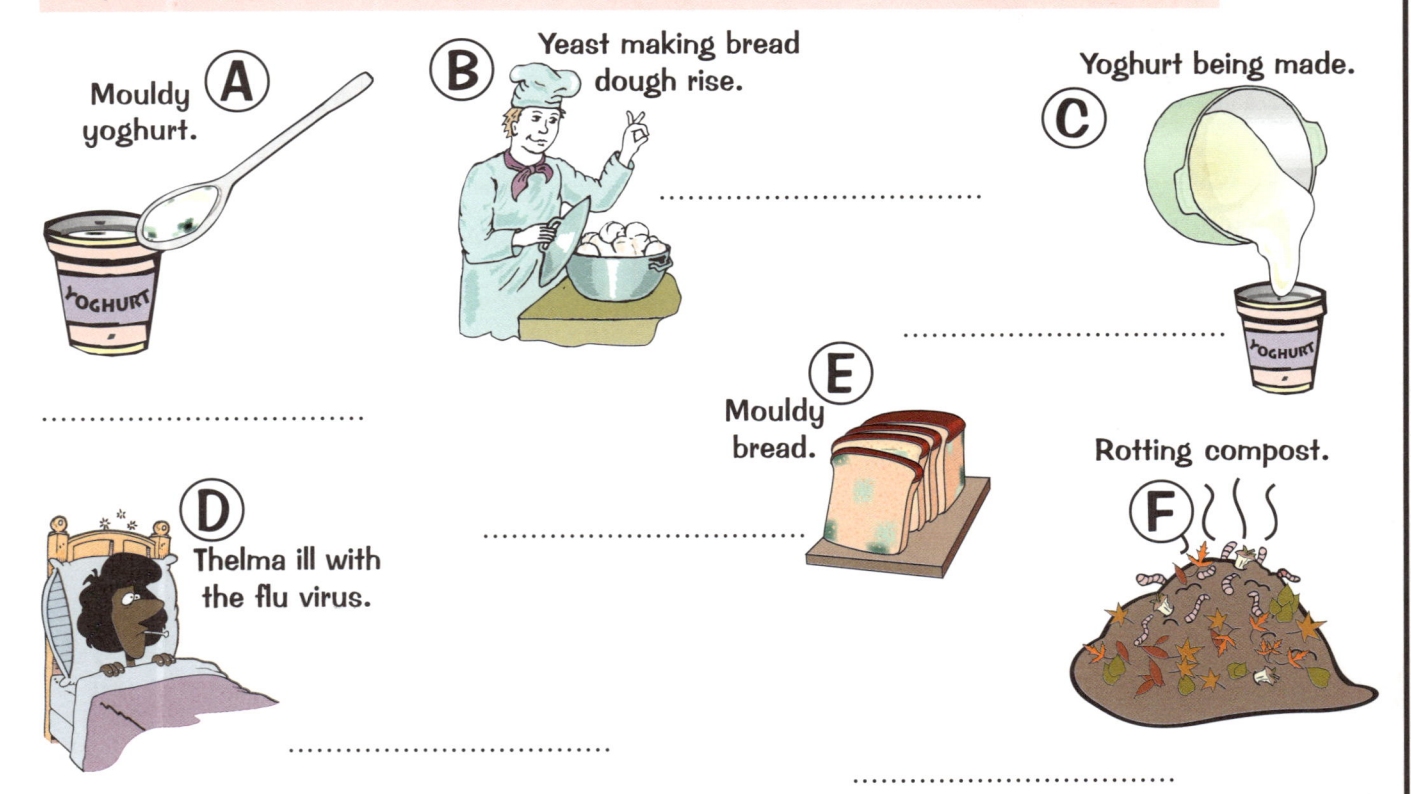

A — Mouldy yoghurt.
B — Yeast making bread dough rise.
C — Yoghurt being made.
D — Thelma ill with the flu virus.
E — Mouldy bread.
F — Rotting compost.

There are helpful micro-organisms.................

There's one big thing to remember from this page — <u>micro-organisms aren't always bad</u>. When they make you ill, that's bad — but the ones that help make yoghurt or make bread rise are great.

Useful Micro-Organisms

There are loads and loads of different micro-organisms, just like there are loads of different birds and animals. Some micro-organisms are dangerous — they can give people diseases, but some are really useful and you can use them to make food, beer and wine.

Q1 Have a think about the micro-organisms in this table, and put a tick under HARMFUL or HELPFUL for each one.

	harmful	helpful
flu virus		
compost decomposers		
yeast in bread		
bacteria in yoghurt		
bread mould		

Michael wasn't being very helpful either.

Q2 Read this passage about cheese production, and then answer the questions below.

From Milk to Cheese

After cows are milked, tankers take the milk to a dairy. The milk is heated up to a high temperature, which kills off harmful bacteria — this process is called pasteurization. Next, special bacteria are added, which make the milk thicken and turn sour. The milk is warmed, and it thickens into lumps called curds, and then the watery part of the milk is drained off. Salt is added to the curds, which are then pressed and moulded into the right shape. The curds then have to be left in a cool place to ripen into cheese.

a) What is the process of killing off harmful bacteria called?
....

b) Are the bacteria that are added helpful or unhelpful?
....

c) What do the bacteria that have been added to the milk actually do?
....

d) What are the lumps that are made into cheese called? ....

e) Should the lumps be left in a warm or a cool place to ripen? ....

.... but will they do your homework?...

When micro-organisms are useful, they can be really useful. In fact, you wouldn't be able to have foods like cheese at all if there weren't any useful micro-organisms. And I really love cheese...

Revision — Micro-organisms

Germs, diseases, mould and bacteria. What a lovely page...

Q1 Fill in the gaps in these sentences about micro-organisms, using the words from the mould growing over there...

air cooking germs stomach mouth hands ill feed cleaning

Diseases are caused by .... Germs are micro-organisms that can be carried in the .... and on things you touch. If germs get into your .... they can make you .... Two ways you can prevent this are by washing your .... before touching food and by .... food properly. There are bacteria in your .... which can rot your teeth. You can stop this happening by .... your teeth to remove the bacteria and bits of food that bacteria could .... on.

Q2 I took this cheese out of the fridge on Monday and left it in the airing cupboard for a week. I drew pictures of the cheese on Monday, on Wednesday and then again on Sunday.

a) Which picture is which? (Label them Monday, Wednesday and Sunday.)

b) I had another block of cheese that I left in the fridge for a week while the first block was in the airing cupboard. Why wasn't there any mould on this block of cheese?

....

c) Write down another way to keep food fresh, apart from putting it in a fridge.

....

Q3 Fill in the gaps in this sentence about how things decay.

Micro-.................... feed on rubbish and release methane as ....

The rubbish eventually .... into nothing.

Phil wondered why no one would swap sandwiches with him.

Q4 Micro-organisms can be useful. Which of these processes need micro-organisms to work? (Tick the ones that do).

Cooking vegetables ☐   Making cheese and yoghurt ☐   Making wine and beer ☐   Making paper aeroplanes ☐

Making bread rise ☐   Lighting fires ☐   Making compost ☐

De-cay — de letter dat comes after de J in de alphabet...

Micro-organisms — they're good, they're bad, they're ugly. That's about all there is to say.

Adding Solids to Water

Imagine putting a spoonful of sugar into a cup of tea. The sugar seems to disappear, but it's still in the tea — you can taste it. The sugar has <u>dissolved</u> in the tea. Sneaky...

Angelica's mixing up some new potions. She wants to know what she can dissolve and what she can't, and she's hoping something will 'react'. Reacting means it will do something exciting, like fizz, or form a new solid. She's putting various things in water, in her cauldron, to see what happens.
To make it a fair test, Angelica's using fresh water every time. The water's cold because her fire's gone out.

The table below tells you what happened to each of the things on the right when Angelica put them into her cauldron.

Solid	What happened...
Sugar	The grains gradually disappeared.
Sand	The grains sank to the bottom of the cauldron.
Purple powder paint	The water turned purple.
Iron filings	The filings sank to the bottom.
Sherbet	The water fizzed and spluttered.
Stock cubes	The water turned brown and smelt of stock.

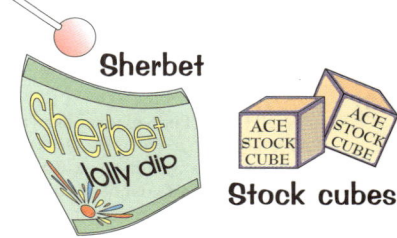

Q1 Which solids dissolved in the water?

....

Q2 Which solids didn't dissolve but just stayed at the bottom of the cauldron?

....

Q3 One kind of solid behaved differently from the rest — which one was it?

....

Q4 What's it called when this happens?   ....

Which page is this — it's the witch page...

Dissolving things is dead useful — it's how you make <u>tea sweet</u>, and how you can get a mug of tasty, comforting tomato soup from a spoonful of <u>odd-looking granules</u>. Lovely.

Adding Solids to Water

If you threw a brick into a swimming pool, it'd stay there until someone <u>took it out</u>. But some things don't just sit there and they don't dissolve — they <u>react</u> instead. Generally, that means they do something a bit more exciting.

Q1 Angelica's put four more different solids in her cauldron of water and stirred them. Write out what's happened underneath each picture.

Salt

....

....

Coffee powder

....

....

Marbles

....

....

Plaster of Paris — This has gone hard

....

....

Q2 Group the four solids by writing their names in the table below.

Will dissolve	Nothing happens	Will react

Angelica would have to buy a new cauldron.

Cut knee? — Go to Paris for a plaster...

It's pretty important to know <u>whether</u> things react if you put them in water. Imagine if you added something to a stew and it suddenly <u>exploded</u> — you'd look pretty funny without any eyebrows...

Adding Solids to Other Liquids

Some things won't react in water but <u>will</u> react in <u>other liquids</u>. A piece of chalk might do <u>nothing</u> in a swimming pool but it'd <u>perk up</u> a bit in a bubbling vat of acid.

This time, Angelica is going to try dissolving things in some other liquids — lemon juice and vinegar as well as water. She's going to use baking soda, sugar and iron filings.

Water   Lemon juice   Vinegar

Q1 Angelica stirs each solid into each liquid. Look at each cauldron, then write underneath it what's happening.

Cauldrons 1-3:
Solid = baking soda

1.   2.   3.

....

Cauldrons 4-6:
Solid = sugar

4.   5.   6.

....

Cauldrons 7-9:
Solid = iron filings

7.   8.   9.

....

Q2 Write each cauldron's number in the correct box in the table below.

Solid will dissolve in liquid	Nothing happens	Solid and liquid will react

Hmm... lemon juice, vinegar — where's the mustard?

Lemon juice and vinegar are actually <u>acids</u> — that's why they taste so sharp. They're not too strong, so they're not dangerous, but they're strong enough to react with metals like <u>iron</u>.

Separating Mixtures

When you mix a solid with water, you can <u>separate</u> them again afterwards by filtering — as long as the solid hasn't <u>dissolved</u> in the water or <u>reacted</u> with it.

Q1 Circle the right words to finish off this paragraph about filtering.

You can SEPARATE / MAKE a mixture of sand and water by fi[ltering]. That's because the water fits through the holes in the filter paper, but the bits of sand are too BIG / SMALL to go through. You CAN / CAN'T separate a solution of salt and water by filtering because the particles of SALT / WATER break down into really tiny bits — so they just PASS THROUGH / GET STUCK IN the holes in the filter paper.

Q2 Circle the right words to finish these sentences about my evaporation experiment.

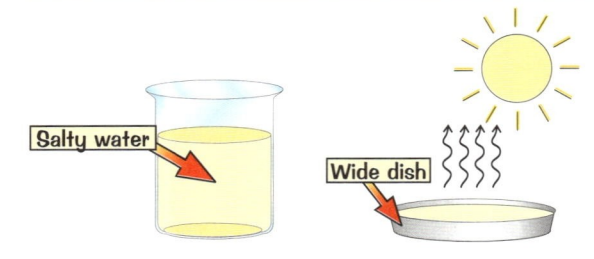

When you mix salt with water, it DISSOLVES / DISAPPEARS. When you heat up the solution of salt and water, the SALT / WATER starts to FREEZE / EVAPORATE. The tiny particles of SALT / WATER don't evaporate — they stay behind. Once all the SALT / WATER has evaporated, all that's left in the container is SALT / WATER. One way to collect the water that's evaporated is by holding a mirror above it. The water FREEZES / CONDENSES into water droplets on the cold surface, and runs off into another container.

Q3 Tick the box underneath the mixtures that you could separate by filtering.

sand in water   salty water   coffee   chalk powder in water   tea

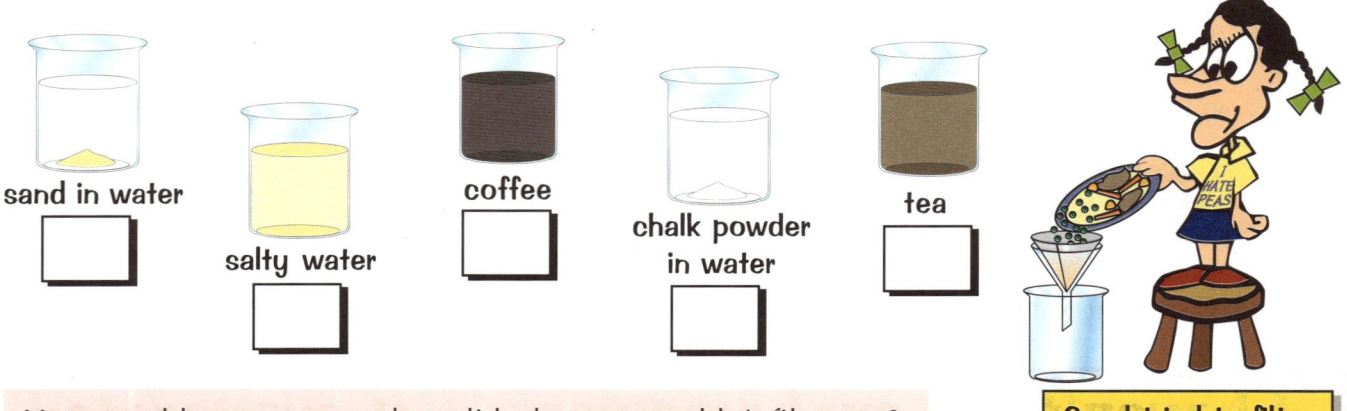

Carol tried to filter her peas out of her Sunday dinner.

Q4 How would you separate the solids that you couldn't filter out?

....

Separating Mixtures

Sometimes when you mix things together, they can be changed back to how they started — that's called a <u>reversible change</u>.

Mixing sand and water is a reversible change. I did an experiment by putting sand in water to make a mixture. Here's a picture of it.

Water   Sand   →   Sand added to water.   →   Sandy water mixture.

Q1 Now I want to reverse the change. Fill in the middle picture in the diagram with a good method for separating the sand and water, and write a description of your method.

Method:

....

....

....

Q2 Is dissolving salt in water a reversible change? ....

If you answered NO, why can't it be reversed? If you answered YES, how can it be reversed?

....

Q3 You know how to separate salt or sand from water, but what about separating a mixture of salt, water <u>and</u> sand? Write SAND, SALT or WATER under the stage where each one is separated out.

Sand   Salt   Water   Cold surface   Burner

....

Q4 Is dissolving sand and salt in water a reversible change? ....

I haven't got my homework — it evaporated...

Reversible changes are great — if you decide you didn't want them mixed, you can <u>separate</u> them again. BUT remember you separate things <u>differently</u> depending on whether they're <u>dissolved</u> or not.

Mixes Involving Irreversible Reactions

Sometimes when you mix two things together they <u>react</u> with each other to produce something new. It'll often <u>bubble</u> or <u>fizz</u> while it's doing it, or sometimes the mixture will go <u>hard</u>.

Q1 Look carefully at this picture of iron filings in lemon juice.
Put a tick next to the sentence which describes what's happening.

☐ The lemon juice used was fizzy and bubbled even before the iron filings were added.

☐ The lemon juice and iron filings are reacting together to produce a gas, which escapes as bubbles.

☐ The iron filings are exploding like bombs making the lemon juice fizz.

Lemon juice and iron filings

Q2 Miriam loves experimenting. Here are pictures of some tests she did.

Baking soda and vinegar

Describe what is happening in the picture.

....

....

Can this change be reversed? ....

What are the bubbles and why are they there?

....

....

....

Lemon juice and washing soda

Describe what is happening in the picture.

....

....

Can this change be reversed? ....

What are the bubbles and why are they there?

....

....

....

Indigestion tablets and water

Describe what is happening in the picture.

....

....

Can this change be reversed? ....

What are the bubbles and why are they there?

....

....

....

So I'm allowed to react badly in the car?..........

Reactions are definitely the most <u>interesting</u> thing that can happen when you mix two things. I've even seen TV shows where a scientist mixed two <u>clear</u> liquids, and they turn bright <u>green</u>.

Mixes Involving Irreversible Reactions

Not <u>all</u> the changes that happen when you mix things together are reversible. Quite a lot of them are irreversible changes — that's another way of saying they only go <u>one-way</u>.

These pictures show an experiment that Miriam did to find out what happens when you mix plaster of Paris with water.

After she'd mixed them together and left them for a while, the mixture turned solid and she couldn't turn it back, or get her spoon out. This is called an <u>irreversible</u> change.

Q1 Miriam tried mixing cement with water next. It formed a solid like the plaster, and she couldn't separate it back into water and cement. Is this a reversible or irreversible change?

This change is ....

Miriam decided that it wasn't a good idea to stir things with her hand.

Q2 Here are pictures of 3 more mixtures Miriam made by adding things to water and stirring them vigorously. Answer the questions for each picture.

a) Describe what is happening.

b) Say whether a new substance has been produced or not. (YES / NO)

c) Say whether the mixture can be split into the two original substances. (YES / NO)

d) Say whether it's a REVERSIBLE or IRREVERSIBLE change.

Sherbet and water
a) ....
b) .... c) .... d) ....

Sand and water
a) ....
b) .... c) .... d) ....

Plaster of Paris and water
a) ....
b) .... c) .... d) ....

.......'cause I can just get my Dad to reverse it...

If a change is <u>irreversible</u>, it means you <u>can't turn it back</u> again. You can't take a piece of chocolate cake and separate it into butter and flour and sugar and cocoa — it's just not possible.

Changes Due to Heating

If you heat something up it might <u>change</u>. Sometimes things can be <u>changed back</u> — but sometimes they <u>can't</u>. This page should help you get what it's all about.

Q1 What happens to water if you heat it to a high enough temperature?

....

Q2 a) Is this a reversible change? ....

This is how Doug changes if you heat him up enough.

b) If you said yes, would you reverse it by heating it up or by cooling it down? If you said no, why can't you reverse it?

....

Q3 a) I've collected together a lot of different things and now I'm going to stick them all in the oven for an hour. Write next to each item what will happen to it in the oven.

cake mix ....

chocolate ....

margarine ....

bread dough ....

candle wax ....

raw egg ....

unfired clay ....

Heating things means doing something to make them hotter, not setting fire to them.

b) Which things from part a) can you most easily get back?

....

c) How can the changes be easily reversed? (Circle) the right answer.

Heat the objects up even more. **Leave the objects in a warm place.** **Let the objects cool down by putting them in a fridge.**

The heat is on — time for a change...

Most things change when you <u>heat</u> them up, but only some can be <u>changed back</u> afterwards. It's lucky that some foods cook when they're heated up — raw eggs <u>really</u> don't taste very good at all.

Changes Due to Cooling

So things often change if you heat them up — but <u>cooling things down</u> can also change them.

Q1 What happens to water if you cool it?

....

Q2 Is this a reversible change? If so, how would you reverse it? If not, why can't you reverse it?

....

....

Andy got the wrong idea when Johnny said 'act cool'.

Q3 a) I'm going to put all these things inb the freezer to cool them down. Write next to each item what will happen to it in the freezer.

potatoes ....

carrot ....

milk ....

peas ....

oven chips ....

orange juice ....

broccoli ....

b) Which of the changes from part a) can be easily reversed, and how?

....

....

c) Fill in this table to show how many of the changes from this and the last page were reversible.

	Number of reversible changes
Changes due to heating	
Changes due to cooling	

d) Are changes more likely to be reversible if they are caused by heating or cooling?

....

Don't look now — I'm just changing...

If you heat some things up, you can change them <u>back</u> to how they were before by cooling them down. But some things <u>won't</u> change back at all. It depends on exactly what they're made from.

Burning Makes New Materials

When you burn wood you can see flames, smoke and ash.
Gases are produced too — but you <u>can't see</u> them.

Q1 Fill in the labels on this picture with the words in the bubble.

FLAMES   WOOD   ASH   GAS   SMOKE

Sabrina and Bill are doing an experiment to see what happens when they burn different materials. Here's their results table.

Type of material	Bits of plastic	Fabric	Coal	Paper
What happened when it was burned?	Plastic starts to melt. Small amount of ash. Nasty smell. Smoke.	Small flame. Lots of ash. Nasty smell. Smoke.	Faint bluish flame. Some ash. Smell. Smoke.	Flame. Lots of ash. Smell. Smoke.

Q2 When each of the four things was burnt, a gas was produced. How can you tell from the results that a gas was produced? (Handy hint: it's <u>not</u> to do with smoke.)

....

Q3 Other than gas, write down what else was produced in the experiment.

....

Q4 For each change from Q1 put a tick if it is reversible or a cross if it isn't — and then explain why.

Plastic ☐ ....

Fabric ☐ ....

Coal ☐ ....

Paper ☐ ....

<u>Sideburns — sounds a bit dangerous...</u>

If you burn things they <u>don't just disappear</u> — they turn into other stuff like gas or ashes. The bad news is that you can't shove everything back together to how it was before — it's <u>irreversible</u>.

Burning Makes New Materials

It's not just <u>solid</u> things that will burn — some liquids and gases will, too.

Q1 Take a look at these substances, and (circle) the ones that will burn.

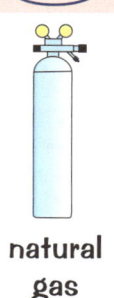

water   coffee   natural gas   paraffin   orange juice   vegetable oil

Q2 I've lit a candle to see what happens as it burns down.

a) After a while there's liquid around the wick — what is it?

....

b) After a couple of hours, the level of the wax has gone down. Why has that happened?

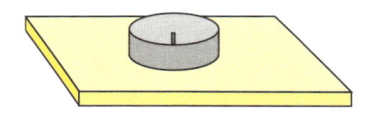

....

....

c) After a while longer, the metal container is completely empty and the flame goes out. Do you think it's possible to reverse the change and bring back the wax?

....

Q3 Write down one possible new substance that could have been produced from the wax burning. ....

Q4 Tick the sentence that describes the change when you burn something.

The change is reversible. ☐

You can burn anything for as long as you want. ☐

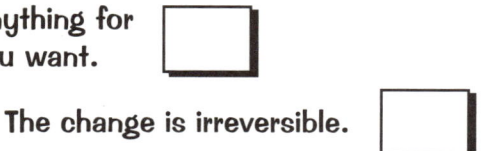

The change is irreversible. ☐

Todd made all sorts of new materials by burning all his meals.

Don't burn money — you'd turn cash to ash...

Things like wax can be <u>liquid</u>, but they still <u>burn</u>. If you burn something you'd better be sure you don't need it any more, because once it's gone, it's <u>really</u> gone — you can never change it back.

Burning is Dangerous

Burning is <u>dangerous</u> — if one thing catches fire, it can <u>set light</u> to other things. Some things burn more easily than others. Things that burn easily often have <u>labels</u> warning people — like this pillow and this armchair.

Q1 Kate is trying to decide which coat to wear for Bonfire Night. Her red coat has this label on it — her blue coat doesn't. Which coat should she wear?

....

Q2 Circle four fire hazards that you can see in this room.

Q3 Here are three sets of gloves. Pair A burns very easily, pair B burns quite easily and pair C does not burn easily. Draw labels on the two more dangerous pairs, to warn people that they could be dangerous.

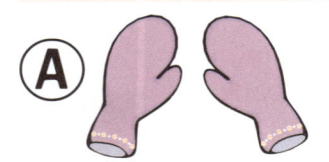

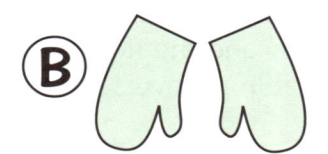

A   B   C

Q4 Look at this winter bonfire and circle five things that you think should be made of flame-resistant material (so they don't catch fire easily).

You'll be burning to do this page...

This is common sense, really — if something is labelled '<u>flammable</u>', it'll <u>burn easily</u>, so be careful with it if it's near any flames. ('Flammable' sounds a bit like '<u>flame</u>', so it's easy to remember.)

Revision Questions

Oh no, the end of the book — the very last page. But not to worry, I've bunged in as much as I could possibly manage. Get your teeth into these questions...

Q1 What will happen to each of these solids when added to water?
Write 'will dissolve', 'will react', or 'won't dissolve' on the dots next to each one.

Chalk dust: .... Sugar: ....

Baking soda: .... Sherbet: ....

Q2 After adding a liquid to a solid, what kind of a change is it when:
a) you can separate them again afterwards, and b) you can't separate them?

a) .... b) ....

Q3 Write next to the following mixtures if they need to be 'filtered', 'evaporated' or 'both' to separate the water from the solid. Write 'irreversible' if they can't be separated again.

A Water and plaster of Paris.
....

B Salt, sand and water.
....

C A sugary cup of tea.
....

D Water and green powder paint.
....

Q4 Draw arrows to the right words to complete these sentences about burning.

1) When I burn fabric: no new material is produced.   a magic trick.

2) I can tell there's gas produced because: I can smell it.
                                                                      reversible.
3) This change is: irreversible.
                                          ash, smoke and gases are produced.

Q5 My new pair of neon-pink nylon flares burn very easily. Draw a warning label for them in this empty box.

When Darren annoyed her, Harriet used her new spell. Darren hoped this was a reversible change...

Time for a change — time for a breather, aah...

You should have had no problems with this page, but flick back through the book and check things if you're not sure. Now you've finished all this stuff, I reckon you've earned yourself a break...

Index

A
acid 3, 15
airtight packaging 5

B
bacteria 2, 3, 10, 11
   Bertie the Bacteria 10
biodegradable 7
bread 4, 11
   bread dough 8, 10, 20
burning 22-24

C
cauldron 13-15
changes
   irreversible 18-20, 24
   reversible 17, 19, 21
cheese 11
chicken pox 2
compost 10, 11
condensing 16
cooking 20
cooling 21
coughing 2
cowpox 1

D
dangerous stuff 24
decay 1, 5-7, 10
   tooth decay 3
decomposers 7, 10
disease 1, 10
   gum disease 3
   infectious diseases 2
   spread of disease 2
dissolving 13-16
drying food 5

E
Edward Jenner 1
evaporating 16

F
filtering 16
fire
   flammable materials 24
   flame-resistant material 24
fizzing 13, 18
flu virus 10, 11

food
   cheese 11
   drying food 5
   food hygiene 5
   pickling food 5
   smelly and horrible food 4
freezer 4, 5, 21
fridge 4, 5

G
gas (methane) 7
germs 1, 2
   germs carried in the air 2
   how germs are passed on 2
green and fluffy sandwiches 5
gum disease 3

H
heating 20
hygiene, food 5

I
infectious diseases 2
insects 2
irreversible changes 18-20, 24

J
Jenner, Edward 1

L
landfills 7
liquids 15
Louis Pasteur 1
lumps of curd 11

M
measles and mumps 2
meat (keeping raw and cooked
     meat apart) 5
methane gas 7
micro-organisms 1-5, 7, 8, 10, 11
   useful micro-organisms 7, 10, 11
milk 11
mixing 19
mould 4, 10
   blue mouldy bits 5
mouth 3

O
oven 20
   oven gloves 24

P
Pasteur, Louis 1
pasteurization 11
packaging (airtight) 5
pickling food 5

R
reacting 13-15, 18
reversible changes 17, 19, 21
rubbish tips 6, 7

S
sandwiches (green and fluffy) 5
separating 16
smallpox 1
smelly and horrible food 4
sneezing 2
solids 15, 19
sticky slime 3
sugar 3, 8

T
tips (rubbish tips) 6, 7
tooth decay 3

U
'Use by' date 5

V
vaccines 1
virus 1
   flu virus 10, 11

W
warmth 9
washing your hands 2, 5
water 13-17, 19

Y
yeast 8-11
   Yeastenders 9
yoghurt 10, 11